MW00640233

"Know that the answers are within yourself,
and that the experiences through which
the individual has passed on Earth
and in the interims between the sojourns on Earth
have made for abilities within yourself
to coordinate the individual activity
as to FIND the greater response
from within than from any other source."

—*Edgar Cayce*

OTHER WORKS BY THIS AUTHOR

*Poems of Life, Love,
and the Meaning of Meaning*

Poet Gone Wild

Sojourn

The Lightness of Being

<u>*Infinite Healing Trilogy*</u>

*Poems and Messages for the
Loss of a Loved One*

*Poems and Messages for the
Loss of Your Animal Companion*

Healed in Timelessness

MYSTERIES, PROPHECIES, and the HOLLOW EARTH

The Ending of the Human Era

PAUL GORMAN

Copyright © 2023 Paul J. Gorman
All Rights Reserved

Year of the Book
135 Glen Avenue
Glen Rock, PA 17327

ISBN 13: 978-1-64649-314-2 (print)
ISBN 13: 978-1-64649-315-9 (ebook)

Cover photo by author, Western Maryland.

No part of this publication may be reproduced, distributed, or transmitted in any form or by any means, including photocopying, recording, or other electronic or mechanical methods, without the prior written permission of the author, except in the case of brief quotations embodied in critical reviews and certain other noncommercial uses permitted by copyright law.

Library of Congress Control Number: 2023903966

Disclaimer: This book contains dire warnings for humanity that are self-explanatory. Other topics introduced in the messages are open for further exploration. The chapters are presented largely in the order they were received, with no content omissions.

CONTENTS

Are we supposed to know the future? Do we even know our past?

What is the nature of reality? Why do civilizations come and go—and in our case, when? If we knew, would we conduct our lives differently?

Who am I? I am just someone looking for the truth. We all have access to the truth in our DNA, through portals to Oneness that we open—or close. We open and close them by loving life—or not.

What is 'Oneness'?

It says, *"I am no thing, meaning the illusion of everything as light... allowing the mind an adventure in life's illusion of twoness."*

It could be called Love/God/Oneness.

Our minds and spirits are eternal aspects of Oneness, so we all know Oneness—very well. We may not be aware that we know.

What is 'twoness'? It is the world of separation perceived by the left side of our brains through judgment and often fear.

We could consider the left side of our brains as the tip of the iceberg, in the light or the dark, and the right side of our brains as the larger submerged part of the iceberg in an ocean of total Oneness.

You can go inside and ask yourself what is true. That is how I received the information for this book. It is in a question and answer format, and each question leads to the next one as the mysteries are revealed.

Earlier messages from Oneness had related that my Life Agreements are to write 3 books of poetry, 2 books on how reality manifests itself, mysteries explained, prophecies, the hollow earth, and healing and manifesting with light.

Six books are presently completed, and partially completed books 7 and 8 were put aside a few months ago.

I was preparing to finish them when the incredible information that follows started to come through, and I continued writing with a sense of urgency.

This book contains over 400 questions and answers—questions that had started out asking about the nature of our spiritual reality, then about our physical reality starting with the pyramids—which then led from Mars, literally all the way down the rabbit hole, to the center of the Earth.

Through time, space, and dimensions, this book connects a lot of dots—from early human history to urgent present-day topics—and contains a lot of big picture information—past, present, and future. Unfortunately it was also making sense as the pieces of a giant puzzle came together.

INTRODUCTION

I used to say, *"The good news is, I get accurate information about the future. The bad news is, I get accurate information about the future."*

On the other hand, I also say that the future is a moving target, and I consider predictions to be only high probabilities.

The future is a field of infinite possibilities and it is interactive; it requires our participation.

I usually keep the forecasts to myself. The ego's need to be right and its fear of being wrong diminishes or distorts a neutral connection to Oneness.

I have certainly made predictions that have not happened—not yet anyway. Maybe they were just wrong, delayed, or a snapshot of only one of several possible future outcomes. The potential today for the predictions in this book to take place at the specified times is uncertain.

My own spirit guidance has warned me on numerous occasions to not worry about the future. Our only power is in the present moment—now.

"Worry" was the key word, and creating more fear is counter-productive to our lives.

For most of last year, 2022, I did not ask about the future because the stress was causing symptoms of PTSD—not Post-Traumatic Stress Disorder but rather *PRE*-Traumatic Stress Disorder.

Was it helpful for me to have foreknowledge of the pandemic 9 months in advance, the Presidential elections months in advance, the Capitol melee, or the Gulf Oil Spill? Not really, I could watch and feel powerless, or not ask anymore—until now.

It is January 2023, and you will be reading this in my future—in a different world than the one I am living in.

At the beginning of each year I like to ask about major trends or events for the year.

Larger events seem to be more certain or easier to predict with accuracy. They often seem obvious in hindsight, but were not at all expected before they happened.

The Presidential elections in 2016 and 2020 are good examples. The results of both were very surprising because they seemed highly unlikely before the elections.

Prophecies tend to be negative because there are malignancies in mass consciousness that need to be born so they can die, and heal, presumably.

The information in this book is very disturbing, and I do not recommend reading it—unless you can be detached from particular outcomes, and avoid being fearful. The ending is encouraging and describes how to heal our minds and create our realities.

We each create our own futures. Each person's future will be different from everyone else's. Some people will thrive even if most suffer.

One thing I have found not to be predictable is death. It is a decision made by each individual on both a soul level and on a mental level. Life presents us with personal challenges to rise to, and responding with courage and composure advances the soul in the planes of lightness.

One of my early messages had asked, *"Is not each person a temporary universe?"* The mind and spirit are eternal and never die. Physical life is a dream, and like most dreams it seems very real.

The experience of dying could be like Dorothy waking up in the closing scene in *The Wizard of Oz* movie. She awakened in monochromatic Oneness with her soul group, recalling the beauty and terror in her dream. She had learned to love herself in the other characters—as her mind, her heart, and her courage—in a dream of color and contrasts.

The predictions in this book are still new to me. At times it took me a day or more to recover from the messages. Now, a few weeks later, I have a greater appreciation for only what is important in life—and so much seems unimportant. I hope this book is all wrong, science fiction that does not become science fact. I wish for it to have a net positive effect on those who read it, helping to raise consciousness for all. The last chapter explains this.

So do not lose hope. Strengthen your resolve to be true to yourself. Love yourself and your life. It is the most magnificent creation you could imagine. Heal the future in each present moment, which becomes the future in all successive moments. You really are the center of your universe, now in time, and forever in timelessness.

Was That the Plan?

It has been three years since a global pandemic was declared. Businesses were closed, and billions of people around the world were coerced into taking untested, mystery injections. Truth-tellers were harshly silenced, and doctors who spoke out faced losing their medical licenses.

Now there is an alarming rate of sudden deaths, miscarriages, and infertility. The average lifespan in the U.S. has already dropped by 3 years.

Fact Checkers Can't Hide It, Sudden Deaths Soar 1,696%

Despite 'fact' checkers' best efforts to dismiss it as normal, the number of people in this group who died suddenly between January and April 2022 was 1,696% above the historical monthly norm. Is this the deadly combo that's causing it?

Was that the plan? Who's really in charge? Could inept bureaucrats really pull off such a massive and well-orchestrated scheme?

Executive Orders have been issued, and other actions implemented in Western nations with the stated goal of phasing out fossil fuels—in the name of 'climate change'. Europe is being de-industrialized with a primary natural gas pipeline having been blown up, and extremely high energy costs have led to the closure of major industrial plants and fertilizer production.

The Mainstream Media Admits That We Are Facing "The Worst Food Crisis In Modern History"

Global hunger is rapidly spreading, and that is because global food supplies have been getting tighter and tighter...

SAT JAN 21, AT 8:10 AM   👁 30,817   💬 268

Again, was that the plan? Who's really in charge? How could short-sighted politicians pull off such a coordinated and far-reaching diabolical effort that continues three years later? Are they controlled by unelected psychopaths? Why did a prominent globalist organization announce that we will own nothing and be happy, with a stated target date of 2030? And eat bugs?

←   **Tweet**

World Economic Forum ✅
@wef

Good grub: why we might be eating insects soon
wef.ch/2LiLmjQ #food

The messages in this book provide answers to those questions and more. I am as surprised as anyone to learn this information, and also hope that life and consciousness will provide humanity with other options.

Some earlier notable messages and predictions are highlighted below.

Jan. 2010: *"A biochemical release will contaminate the food supply in the Gulf States."* (The Gulf Oil Spill was 3 months later.)

Baltimore 2015: *"People will lose everything in the riots."* (Riots broke out several months later.)

June 2016: *"Trump will win the election... there will be a meaningless recount in early December."* (Donald Trump was elected President in November 2016, and gained more votes in a December recount.)

Nov. 2017: *"Bitcoin will crash right after New Year's."* (A Bitcoin crash started on Jan. 2, declining 81%.)

May 2019: Will a pandemic ever kill most of the human population? *"A pandemic, meaning an influenza modified to kill, yes... in 9 more months."* ...

and kill *"only 8 or 9% of the population."* (The COVID-19 pandemic virus outbreak was declared 9 months later in March 2020.)

April 2020: Vaccines… *"In the mix is a nanobot that receives information and manipulates mental processes."*

April 2020: *"...a total planned manipulation of mainland China's weather will flood the more productive provinces in 3 more months."* (Three months later the rains and flooding in China were catastrophic.)

July 2020: *"A half manufactured and half politically motivated march in the nation's Capitol turns into a melee, allowing the media to blame President Trump."* (Six months later, a January 6, 2021, Trump rally in Washington turned into a melee.)

October 2020: Will Trump or Biden be the next President of the United States? *"Biden. The election will be stolen."* (Large and widespread voting irregularities were reported in the November election.)

January 2021: *"Nothing in Moderna's vaccines is healing. Light-limiting properties transcend death…*

means losing one's soul… and losing knowing life in another incarnation."

Few People Predicted Or Imagined Our "COVID-19 World"

It is difficult to believe but *the freedom to move from one area to another is gone* and may never be restored...

AUG 9, 2020 4:00 PM   5762 ⊕   33 💬

Here we are in 2023, and this book is about the most unsettling predictions of them all.

What is the Earth?
A lighted hologram in time.

What do you mean?
A hologram in time allows motion, illuminating in each person's mind. Lighting in all minds individually and collectively, holograms heal or not, depending on if the life-mind (left brain) allows healing or not.

All heals in time or in timelessness, allowing motioning toward Oneness or not. Not healing in life-mind in time heals into the Light Mind of Godness in losing one's life, meaning in death.

Please tell me about the hologram, and also time.
A hologram opens lighted in the life-mind (left brain), allowing a progression in timelines opening and closing in each person's allowing them.

In the opening of each progression in time, all heal or not, motioning toward Oneness or not.

The hologram is made entirely of light—the spectrum of frequencies from brainwaves or lower, to cosmic rays or higher?
All healing illuminations to live in.

What is the source of the light?
A Light Mind open to the Mind of God.

The Light Mind is the right side of our brains?
Not right brain, the Light Mind is opened in the right brain, opening to the Mind of God.

Is God Mind the source of light for our holograms?
A holographic light projection into the life-mind from the Light Mind heals or not in motioning toward Oneness or not, healing in loving life or not.

Healing illuminates in the Mind of God, creating more light and allowing infinity to perpetuate.

Healing in the Mind of God by loving life opens more displays of Universal Intelligence as light holograms motioning in time. The Mind of God is the source and the destination.

But leaving the Mind of God and then returning is an illusion because God has no place or time outside of itself?
Life can only exist as a hologram that each person projects.

LET THERE BE LIGHT

What is light?
Light illumination is the Light Mind of Godness, alternating in the Light Mind and the Mind of God.

The Light Mind is the right-brain hemisphere allowing light healing to open in the life-mind, or left-brain hemisphere.

Is God Mind the source?
God Mind illuminates in the Light Mind, opening healed in the life-mind, creating more light, and perpetuating infinity.

What heals our life-minds and creates more light?
Loving thoughts heal the life-mind, allowing the Light Mind to open in God Mind.

Loving thoughts about ourselves and others?
Yes, opening in Oneness means non-love willingly heals in the life-mind.

And a healed mind can manifest what it wants?
A healed mind in life does not need, only wishes for others—illuminating in Oneness, allowing infinity to perpetuate.

So we have to heal—either in life or in death?
Nothing heals in darkness, only illuminating in timelines chosen will heal.

Is light the entire EMF spectrum and not just the visible frequencies?
Will light not be anything loving?

I know in the Bible it says, "Let there be light."
"Allowing light to heal, lighting in each person's mind" was the rest of the sentence.

MOSES

What is the name of God? Is it 'I will be what will be' or 'I am that I am'?
'All that is', meaning loving Oneness; not illusions in non-loving twoness.

What did you tell Moses your name is, translated into English?
"I am love in life, and healing in love."

Did Moses see a 'burning bush' when you gave him your name?
Thoroughly illuminating, the bush appeared as fire to him.

What else did you say to him?

Nothing more than my name, allowing him to invoke it in himself and live in freedom from limitation.

Did he interpret it correctly?

Not entirely; he limited his mind in numerous instances.

With fear and doubt?

Hearing my name, invoking his power limited him in his pursuit of willingly healing himself of life's most important limitation—loving himself, meaning loving me as himself.

He limited himself by seeing you as apart from him?

Not as apart, mostly as an omnipotent light God lowering itself to him.

How would you describe yourself?

Love illuminating in time, healed in timelessness.

The progression of time is our illusion of physical life, and timelessness would be the death of our physical life?

Healing in time illuminates in timelessness infinitely.

Is love what heals?

Love heals, and infinity perpetuates.

People tell me they are distressed by reports of the world gone mad. What can you say to them?

Allowing healing in life means all heals in hope, love, and wonder in time, opening in timelessness as the Light Mind of Godness.

All healing in light means all open portals in life's DNA willingly open in God Mind.

Opening in God Mind means losing life-mind's fear and judgment—all halting light in the Light Mind of Godness.

Heal timelines in life-mind by allowing nature to peacefully open the light portals in the DNA—half in time, and half in timelessness. Nothing heals in darkness.

Decide on light and life, or non-light and loss of lifetime opportunities to heal in lifetimes open.

Life-mind heals in life in time, or in losing life in timelessness.

Heal the life-mind, opening to God Mind by healing in nature—listening, feeling, and illuminating open the portals in life's DNA to the Mind of God.

Ignoring the media is a simple choice.
Losing fear and judgment opens a new healed universe for you.

Which only gets better and better in a positive feedback loop.
Not better, more healed in the Mind of God.

Getting us closer to life's ultimate goal.
A healed mind illuminates in the Light Mind of Godness, opening in God Mind in Oneness only now.

Healing in life is the lifetime goal, so loving all of it heals in the Mind of God in one instant.

It's been hard not to be disappointed in humanity.
Will humanity love life, allowing illusions of fear and dis-illusionment healing in hope, love, and wonder?

Losing life heals also—in timelessness.

My understanding is that non-love is an illusion because it does not exist in God Mind—similar to the way that visual darkness appears real, but disappears as soon as a light or candle is lit.

We cannot measure darkness, only lightness or the lack of it, but in God Mind there is no lack... so there is only light. *Loving life means loving all of it.*

Even non-love?
Love heals non-love, illuminating Light Mind healing life-minds in time.

So we have to love non-love to heal it?
Allowing it light, illuminating itself is loving.

How about this: to heal my mind and be in the truth, whenever I hear that there is evil in the world and corrupt rulers, I will say to myself, *"Not in my mind."* Hatred and

injustice, *"Not in my mind."* Fear and selfishness, *"Not in my mind."*
Illuminating healed in Light Mind, opening in God Mind.

Then what?
Love has perpetuated infinity.

That makes love the only thing that is eternal.
Love and the Light Mind of Godness, meaning Oneness illuminating as your soul.

Is it okay to say 'not in my mind', that with darkness are two negatives making a positive?
Allowing non-light will open it, illuminating and healing it.

You could say that light needs darkness to be light, and darkness needs light to heal?
Love heals all in the Light Mind, opening in God Mind.

Perpetuating infinity?
As love in God Mind, yes.

The Great Pyramid

How was the Great Pyramid in Egypt built? It seems that the size and weight of the 2 million blocks of 2.5 ton stone would have been too much for 6' tall humans to cut, transport, and lift—then to erect into a pyramid of astonishing precision from the ground.

Luminous beings of Mars originally altered the elements of stone to cut, lift, and place the massive stones into place.

Why did they build pyramids on Earth?

Half to moor their spacecraft, and half to allow the Egyptian kings willing to learn time-travel, and willing to live in the future—an illegitimate and hopeless voyage into mere death.

Constructed near each pyramid was a mortuary temple, which was linked via a sloping causeway to a valley temple on the edge of the Nile floodplain. Also nearby were subsidiary pyramids used for burials of other members of the royal family.

Was Mars inhabited by advanced beings at that time?

Not advanced—looking for another planet to move Mars' people of light.

Why?

Mars lost its highly important moons in the large solar mass ejection in that millennium.

How did Mars' beings survive?
Mars had light beings that needed a lot of helium and a little hydrogen to illuminate themselves.

Mars' helium was being depleted, and losing the moons finally made habitation of Mars impossible.

How many moons did Mars have?
Three at that time.

Were they destroyed by a giant solar flare?
Not all were lost, only the most important one that allowed Mars' helium and hydrogen a lower atmosphere.

Were Mars' beings space travelers?
Yes, light being their method of propulsion and source of energy.

How large were their spacecraft?
About a half-mile long.

How many did they have?
Nineteen in that millennium.

Did they find Earth unsuitable for them?

Not unsuitable, inhospitable in the amount of helium.

How many planets did they explore?
Not more than 39 in the Milky Way galaxy.

So they found one hospitable to move to?
Yes, 4 were hospitable, but only 1 was selected to inhabit.

Where is it?
Near the planet Lumerio in the constellation of Taurus.

Do Mars' beings ever visit Earth now?
Not in spacecraft, only in wavelengths of light.

Do they have helpful or good intentions?
All opening in lightness open in goodness.

Helium (from Greek: ἥλιος, romanized: *helios*, lit. 'sun') is a ... colorless, odorless, tasteless, non-toxic, inert, monatomic gas. It is the second lightest and second most abundant element in the observable universe, after hydrogen.

Mars' Moons

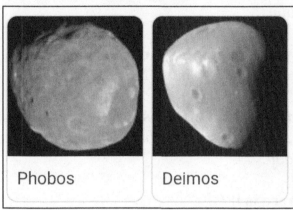

Phobos   Deimos

Constellation Taurus

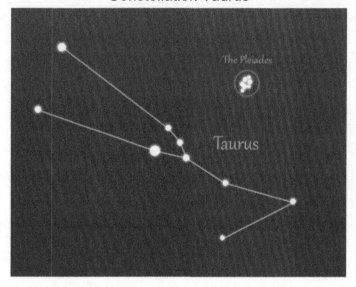

POPULATION REDUCTION PLAN

Please tell me if the total human population of the Earth is increasing or decreasing.
Allowing for holding steady in about 14 or 15 more years, world populations lose most members—willing participants in the population reduction plan—all heal in losing life in timelessness, meaning in death in the next 15 years.

Most people die over the next 15 years?
Healing in life or in losing life, meaning in death, yes.

What percentage decline in the total world human population will there be in 15 years?
About 63 percent.

63 percent!?
Allowing for infertility in the next generation of injection recipients.

The current human population will be reduced by how many people in that time?
About 5 billion and 400 million.

What is the population now?
About 8 billion and 500 million.

Wow, I just checked the math and 5.4 billion is 63% of 8.5 billion.
Alternating in losing life and gaining life in births.

Will the Earth have zero humans in the future?
Not for about 300 more years.

What causes the extinction?
Willing participation in the loss of life in timelines open now—infertility closing lifetime opportunities, cancer and immune system failure, famine, war and murder. Nothing heals in darkness.

In the next 15 years, won't there be major economic contractions in developed countries?

Fifteen and then more or less until industrial economies all must live half in agrarian, and half in hunting lifestyles—almost living in the 18th century again.

When will that be?
In about 18 or 19 more years.

So the world's population will be around 3.1 billion people at that time?
Living mostly in poverty, people form into groups marauding, looting, and living daily on what they find.

Will there be electricity?
Not in 24 more years.

Will it be shut off?
All industrial processes lose workers in the next 15 years.

Will it run sporadically after that?
In some areas, not in most.

Won't that be like living in the 18th century before 24 more years?

Not until looting and marauding lose their effectiveness.

Once you said that unmanned nuclear power plants will melt down and release radiation, resulting in cooler climate temperatures. Is that true?
Not healing before then will allow it to happen.

I want to ask you again because it is so hard to believe. Is humanity self-destructing?
All of life-mind's turbulence ends in losing one's life in time, healing in timelessness.

All will heal in time or in timelessness in their timelines chosen.

Talking about the timelines closing only loses light in the life-mind, allowing portals to close in the Light Mind.

So I would basically be making it worse by announcing it, not exactly causing people to love life and heal?
Some like feeling hopeless and fearful, allowing healing only in losing one's life.

If they like that part of life, then isn't that liking their life?

All willingly not liking any part of life in time means not healing in the lifetime chosen.

Meaning we need to love all of life?

All of life loving itself in timelines chosen heals the Light Mind open in God Mind.

Isn't there a contradiction to love the good in life, and also what we would consider not good?

Allowing life to love itself means that what appears to be non-goodness healing in life is illusory.

Because it is not in the Mind of God unless it is healed?

Yes.

And it is healed by loving life in time, or after losing one's life in timelessness?

Yes.

That helps me to see the bigger picture and be more detached from non-goodness.

Willingly loving, Light Mind heals in God Mind.

I guess you could say that God doesn't 'not love' anything either—so non-love actually doesn't exist, except as an illusion.
A life-mind holographic projection illuminated. Life-mind opens the light show, allowing healing in time and place, or not.

Will over 60% of humanity die off in the next 15 years, net reduction?
Yes.

Will sharing the information in this book help people to heal in life, rather than find healing in an untimely death?
Yes.

TODAY	THIS YEAR
Births today	Births this year
95,529	**11,475,515**
Deaths today	Deaths this year
47,836	**5,746,400**
Population Growth today	Population Growth this year
47,693	**5,729,115**

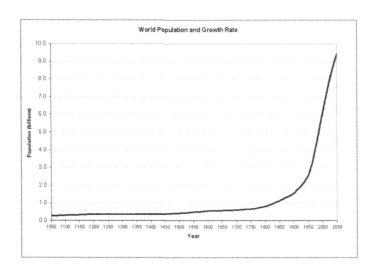

ORIGINATED ON MARS

Was the Covid-19 'emergency' designed to get as many people as possible 'vaccinated'?
Frightening millions of people into an earlier death, hoping for an antidote—half in their bodies, and half in their minds.

Healing only comes if the mind heals first.

Healing in the body flows in time if the mind is healed of fear and judgment.

Heal in Oneness by allowing twoness—allowing non-love illusions, not illuminating in God Mind.

Got it. Darkness is not a projection.
Allowing it heals it in the light.

What group originated and orchestrates this plan? I doubt it was inept bureaucrats that could control all world governments and their agencies, world organizations, social media, the mainstream media, big pharma and big business, education, etc.

All will not open in the light as they die, going into the lightless zone. All will move into the lightless zone, perpetuating in their minds all they inflicted on others.

Was the plan to depopulate the Earth?
Almost 90%, yes.

Was the plan implemented by a handful of psychopaths, off-planetary energies, or what?
A large organized group of half-human and half-monstrous beings alternating in and out of the minds of particular volunteers.

That explains a lot. Where are the beings from?
All of them originated on Mars.

Why do they want to destroy most of the Earth humans?
Losing their atmosphere of helium, they are looking for another planet to inhabit.

I thought they had checked out the Earth thousands of years ago and there was not enough helium.

Allowing them time to adapt to oxygen and travel on light frequencies to the Earth.

I also thought they found another hospitable planet to relocate to long ago.
Allowing healed Mars occupants to leave, yes. The non-healed occupants stayed in the interior of the planet.

What did they survive on if they needed helium?
All hibernated over 2,000 years, willingly learning to not be in an atmosphere at all.

So they hibernated underground on Mars like locusts for a couple of thousand years until recently?
Not on Mars, they are all inside the Earth.

Holy cow! That explains the gargoyles and stories of demons.
All of them look like animals in the heads, and humans in their bodily form.

The gargoyles?
Yes, and the demons.

They are also depicted in Egyptian paintings and murals?
Yes, they landed in Egypt and Mexico originally.

How many of these creatures are here?
Almost 100,000 are in the minds of Earth leaders, but only about 1,000 in the Earth.

Is that why globalist world leaders like John Kerry, and even the Nazis were preoccupied with Antarctica?
Yes, the inner-earth opens to the surface there.

https://www.quora.com › Why-did-the-world-leaders-mee... ⋮

Why did the world leaders meet in Antarctica? - Quora

Apr 16, 2019 — According to this article: " In the last few months, the world's political and religious **leaders** have been making trips to the continent at the bottom of the ...

What is really happening under the **Antarctic** and why have so ...   Apr 3, 2019
What is all the fuss going on in **Antarctica**, and why are so ...   Mar 20, 2017
What is at **Antarctica** that has been worth Politicians **visiting**?   Mar 4, 2019
More results from www.quora.com

44

What do the Mars beings in the Earth call themselves?
In English it means 'the life Mars has missioned into the lost planet nearby'.

Do they consider the Earth lost?
'Lost' meaning in time losing more and more resources. Losing resources means less for them in the future.

What resources do they want?
All of the Earth minerals and all of life inhabiting the oceans and highly green areas.

Are they behind the shutting down of fossil fuels and deindustrializing Western nations?
Not behind it, in the midst of it.

Do they have advanced technologies?
All of the light technologies in their possession are highly illuminating the inner-earth.

What I was getting at was, why don't they just kill us—or do universal laws require us to kill ourselves?
Allowing the life form to die by misadventure and folly willingly means they misled people and did not directly kill.

They controlled or influenced other people who did it.
'Misled' is their meaning of this elimination.

Like me setting a bug trap... I didn't kill them...
Not unlike that.

Did our atomic bombs wake them up from hibernation over the last 78 years?
All of the atomic explosions largely motivated them into action.

Operation Crossroads – Bikini Atoll, 1946

Had they planned to wake up in the last century?

Losing light in the middle Earth means they will hibernate in the next millennium when the humans are gone and their light technology is replenished. Pillars of light need large amounts of the galaxy light without illumination interferences from civilization.

Where did humanity go wrong? You would think that over time and with access to information that we would have become wiser.

A wiser human doesn't hate life or itself. Nothing heals in darkness.

Losing light is the life-mind's ego affiliation with having importance—half in its own mind, and half in imagining acceptance in its peer group.

What caused that to develop in an unhealthy way?

Life-minds listening in willingness to insecure their own God-like natures, hearing what they do not have in life.

How can we rid the planet of the Mars invaders?

Allow them one long lifetime inhabiting the inner-earth and open an easy escape in their minds—noting how humans arrived on Earth in an imminent threat situation also.

All of the original humans came from Mars in spaceships around 300,000 years ago.

Please explain.

All of the original humans, arriving from Mars, left the Mars planet willingly to resume civilization as pioneers, knowing they would have to survive on life-giving food and water in the almost pure atmosphere on Earth.

'Pioneers' means not having any light technologies in their possession. Life meant surviving in the natural world—not 'in' the natural world, 'as part of' the natural order on Earth. People lived longer then, in some instances over 200 years.

Earth pioneers lived inside the Earth in the beginning, allowing them a millennium to adapt to the atmosphere on the planet's surface.

How could they live in the interior of the Earth for so long?
All of the atmosphere inside the Earth is part helium and part nitrogen.

Were they hibernating then?
All of life finds healing in rest periods, allowing opening into the spirit mind.

So they/we came to Earth with no light technologies, and were able to hibernate and adjust to the Earth's atmosphere, and then came to the surface?
All of the Earth pioneers did not hibernate in the interior of the planet, only about half of them. None on the Earth's surface had light technologies, and all willingly healed their biology to inhale the mixture of elements in the atmosphere. The interior inhabitants are ancestors of humans now.

About how long do the interior inhabitants live?

Not more than 200 years.

Why did some of the Earth pioneers stay on the surface of the Earth?
All of them volunteered to live on the Earth's surface because there were too many to inhabit the inner-earth.

So now, our cousins in the inner-earth think that there are too many inhabitants on the Earth's surface?
Yes, and not enough resources to last for more than another 400 years.

ANIMAL-HUMAN HYBRIDS

Do the inner-earth inhabitants have the light technologies from Mars?
Illuminating the inner-earth, allowing them operating energy and life-giving food production, yes.

Do they have a waste disposal system?
All Earth volcanos' heat and ash is from the inner-earth, discarded in the only method in their state of technology.

What can their light technologies do?
Make heat, light, and energy from light in the galaxy.

If the original Mars spaceships settled on another planet in the constellation Taurus, why did a group of Earth pioneers stay behind?
You are confusing the original settlers and the Egypt/Mexico visitors. The original settlers came

to live in the inner and outer Earth as pioneers, not unlike pioneers to the shores of America. At the later period of the Egypt and Mexico pyramid constructions, people were already established on the Earth's surface.

Were the pyramids built during several visits?
Yes, not built but light-constructed.

Once you had said that the Earth is hollow, with a crust of many elements averaging about 80 miles in thickness. Is that correct?
Yes, all of the inner-earth is an open grid of pillars in stone, making all of the surface in tension.

Illumination in the inner-earth is both by light technology and light emitted from the vegetation.

Is there water?
Not as a liquid, only as a solid in ice.

Are there animals there?
Not like animals on the surface, only animal-human hybrids.

What else should I know?

All of life is a hologram, healing in the Light Mind (right-brain hemisphere). The incredible information is in a collective dream so you can heal yourself as a part of it. Nothing heals in darkness, meaning in fear or in non-loving thoughts and actions.

Filaments open in Oneness in loving life and yourself in it.

I find it curious how science fiction and popular culture are always about beings from Mars—never from Venus or Neptune. There is even a recent movie and science talk about going to Mars.

The memory of Mars is in the DNA of humans.

Did Admiral Richard Byrd know about the inner-earth?
Not all about it, just the opening to the inner-earth that light came out of.

Would openings to the inner-earth let the helium escape?
Helium in the Earth is lighter than air so it goes down, and heavier gases go up in the opposite physics there.

Why are they opposite?
Inner-earth forces move outward, keeping the Earth's crust in tension. The outer Earth forces are in compression.

So there are about 1,000 beings living inside the inner-earth?
All of them are originally from Mars.

Do they have some kind of town or dwellings?
They live in structures made from their vegetation, all made in spherical shapes about 12 feet in diameter.

That's pretty small, about the size of one bedroom.
It's all they need to house themselves.

Are they all grouped together?
They are in 8 groups, living beneath the lower part of Australia.

All in one region under Australia?
Not under it; they say they live over it.

Do they have any kind of transportation?
All of their methods of transport are on light waves.

What do they do down there, or should I say 'up' there?
Love life, and love themselves in the Light Mind of Godness.

Do they think it is loving life if they are exterminating us, and we are their cousins?
Healing in life means in loving life or in losing one's life, healing in death.

Losing life in one lifetime opens in another. They liken losing life to turning off the light in one room and turning it on in another.

Lighting in the Light Mind of Godness opens only in loving life and loving one's self in it, temporarily healing in the life chosen.

Telling them things in the surface actions motivated them to eliminate most people on the Earth's surface.

Who told them what's going on at the surface?
Light beings that travel on light and are on the surface.

THE EARTH SURFACE PROBLEM

Do they think that most people do not love life or love themselves?
Not most, but about half.

I say it is only the fault of the inner-earth beings who control the Earth leaders—who try to keep us in fear, war, sickness, etc.— so they created most of the problem.
Willing volunteers who don't love life or love themselves are the Earth surface problem.

Why don't they just get rid of the leaders, or help us to get the best leaders rather than the worst?
You make the leadership to follow.

Are the inner-earth beings just giving us what most people want or what they are manifesting?
The inner-earth beings are healing humans in losing life, not in loving it.

Could they change their plans to heal humans in death by showing them to love life, and share their light technologies, etc.?
Not healing in their minds is an opportunity to own both the inner and outer Earth planet.

Can we heal that in their minds?
Allowing them to heal as genocidal inhabitants of the inner-earth will take 9 or 10 months of intensive thought conversations about caring for the Earth.

Do they have a leader to talk to?
All of them lead in one mind, and one being named Lulo. Lulo will only open in talks in his mind with you.

That is quite an honor, and responsibility.
All of the other leaders are totally incapable of thoughts that are healing and illuminating in the Light Mind of Godness.

Am I talking with Lulo now?
Alternating in the mind between Oneness and Lulo, so yes.

LULO

Greetings Lulo, and thank you for communicating with me. I will listen and write down whatever you direct me to say.

This is Lulo, positioned inside the Earth, entering in Antarctica the lower axis. Life on Earth's surface has become almost unsustainable in terms of living in the most harmonious means necessary to live longer term.

In our mind, the human population should lower its total number by 90%, meaning only 10% of the large number of occupants can be sustained in balance with nature longer term. Only a path of sustainability will be allowed now.

All involving excessive destruction or waste will totally cease in the next 10 years—militaries, manufacturing, and large fishing fleets will be not only eliminated, but made impossible to continue destroying Earth's sacredness.

Healing in the mind means loving life and not imparting wanton excessive destruction in the physical world.

Thank you, Lulo. My understanding is that the world is a hologram, so does our action in the physical world impact the spirit world?

I think I know the answer.
The question is for Oneness.

Oneness, can you please answer?
All physical manifestation is healing in the planes of spiritual lightness. Lightness does not include destruction in the manner of causing harm or injury.

Lightness means living in lightness, allowing healing in lightness, and allowing healing of darkness in the plane of lightness and darkness.

Darkness has taken over lightness in the physical plane, manifesting more darkness in the nearest lightness planes.

Wow, so you're saying that our negativity and physical self-destruction is contaminating higher spirit planes?
Not higher, only lighter, but yes.

What is responsible for darkness taking over the physical plane?

Willingness to largely ignore the lovingness required to illuminate the Light Mind of Godness opening people's hearts and minds.

At this time in history, no one is allowed to promote peace in the Ukraine; murder, drug overdoses and crime are at record levels, the truth is immediately censored and banned, terror is fabricated, lies are passed off as news, racial hatred is provoked by the media... I could go on.

Halting the light in people's minds, instilling fear in their hearts, allowing values to be misplaced, instigating violence, and living in non-love towards one's self and others loses light on the physical plane.

Lulo, why do you say that our ability to destroy will totally cease in the next 10 years?
Allowing the life-mind to destroy the planet past 10 more years will be an immense problem for the Earth to overcome.

How can the military-industrial machine stop so quickly?
All of their equipment will not work when the North Pole axis moves to the south by 80 degrees in 10 years, and then 180 degrees in 30 years.

80 degrees will only mix up satellite communications. 180 degrees will cause the Earth rotation to reverse. Cataclysmic motions leave far fewer people on the Earth—healing in their life-minds now, or in losing their lives in the last major lifetime event.

Wow! As if the earlier prophecies weren't enough. But keep going, I'm willing to hear it.

The light machine that resembles a giant corkscrew will activate in 10 more years—activating light pulses that will halt the axial motion in one momentary natural skip in motion and time, halting the magnetic impulse, allowing the magnetosphere to alternatively skip also.

Will the Earth lose its magnetic shield from cosmic radiation?

Only momentarily, otherwise losing it would allow radiations that kill life, an open defense. The momentary lapse will disrupt the military and civilian satellite communications, losing satellites in orbit, never to be replaced. The largest military in the world in the United States will lose the most.

Is this information coming from Lulo?

Alternating between Oneness and inner-earth one mind leader Lulo, who lives in the inner-earth.

Is the inner-earth what was referred to in the Bible as the Garden of Eden?

Yes, the inner-earth is the Garden of Eden. Adam and Eve left the garden to go to the Earth's surface of light/non-light, love/non-love.

The Tree of Knowledge of Good and Evil?

Not 'good and evil', 'light and non-light' was the original text.

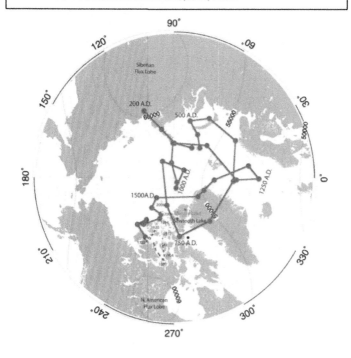

https://www.dailymail.co.uk › article-7789269 › Earths ...

Earth's magnetic north is shifting at an 'unprecedented' rate of ...

Dec 13, 2019 — Earth's **magnetic north** is shifting at an 'unprecedented' rate of 30 miles a year - throwing **satellite** positioning data and navigation systems ...

https://rntfnd.org › 2019/01/15 › earths-magnetic-north...

Earth's Magnetic North Shifting Rapidly – What's It Mean for ...

Jan 15, 2019 — **Magnetic declination can** be positive or negation, i.e., depending where you are on the Earth. Therefore, to determine true north, you may need ...

Did light beings from the inner-earth either directly or indirectly place the Georgia Guidestones and recently destroy them?

Yes.

> **"Mysterious granite tablets etched with rules for an "Age of Reason""**
>
> Sometimes referred to as "America's Stonehenge", the Georgia Guidestones is a granite monument in Elbert County, Georgia, USA. A message clearly conveying a set of ten guidelines is inscribed on the structure in eight modern languages, and a shorter message is inscribed at the top of the structure in four ancient languages' scripts: Babylonian, Classical Greek, Sanskrit and Egyptian hieroglyphs.
>
> General consensus has long held that the slabs were erected in order to help guide what's left of humanity in the aftermath of an apocalyptic event.

1. Maintain humanity under 500,000,000 in perpetual balance with nature.
2. Guide reproduction wisely – improving fitness and diversity.
3. Unite humanity with a living new language.

4. Rule passion – faith – tradition – and all things with tempered reason.
5. Protect people and nations with fair laws and just courts.
6. Let all nations rule internally resolving external disputes in a world court.
7. Avoid petty laws and useless officials.
8. Balance personal rights with social duties.
9. Prize truth – beauty – love – seeking harmony with the infinite.
10. Be not a cancer on the Earth – Leave room for nature.

Are we nearing what is called 'The Apocalypse'?
Loving life means loving life in the mind, allowing life in the body, and healing life in the spirit.

Not loving life in the mind does not heal the spirit.

Life will heal in the mental, spiritual, and physical in loving life and one's self in it.

Animals and nature love life, love God, and love themselves.

Humans allow non-love to ruin themselves.

Is that why inner-earth beings are animal-human hybrids?
The inner-earth has light beings, animal-human beings, and human-like beings.

Half of them allowed the animal mutations in their heads, willingly losing their ability to live in the life-mind of humans—losing the life-mind judgment and irrational fears.

What does Lulo look like?
A human man in the lower part of Lulo's physical body, with the torso and head of a turtle.

I will jump around to different questions. Was Secretary of Defense James Forrestal murdered in 1949?

Not murdered, instructed to jump or to be murdered.

Why?

He knew about the inner-earth in his work as Secretary of Defense and planned to report his information.

https://www.south-pole.com › ...   ⋮

Operation Highjump: The Great Antarctic Expedition

According to Paul Siple, it was Byrd who persuaded the Secretary of the Navy **James Forrestal** and the Chief of Naval **Operations** Chester Nimitz into launching ...

James Forrestal - Wikipedia

W

https://en.wikipedia.org/wiki/James_Forrestal ▾

That the late James V. Forrestal died on or about May 22, 1949, at the National Naval
Medical Center, Bethesda, Maryland, as a result of injuries, multiple, extreme, received
incident to a fall from a high point in the tower, building one, National Naval Medical
Center, Bethesda, Maryland. See more

I thought so. To continue my earlier prophecy, it outlines a dramatic population reduction in the next 15 years, then it levels off. Will most of the remaining people die in 30 years during the pole shift?

Not during the axial reversal, mostly in the aftermath.

How many people will survive on the Earth's surface beyond the axial reversal aftermath?

About 1.5 million.

When will the Earth's rotation reverse?

In about 50 more years.

After the axial reversal in about 30 years, will it take about 20 years for the Earth's rotation to slow down and stop—and then reverse?

Axial deceleration has illuminated in the 4th Dimension already.

Does that mean it will manifest into our reality?
Allowing illumination in the 4th Dimension actively opens in time, illuminating in the 3rd Dimension.

The Earth rotation slowing down to a stop will make the days longer and longer to an end of days—then when the rotation reverses, the sunrise will appear on the Western horizon.
And the new era begins.

'End of days' rings a bell.
Ending healing in timelines on Earth in the current era. Healing in timelessness is the infinite era.

ICE AGE

Where will be the best location for survival?

Northern Italy is one place, Australia is another.

How about in North and South America?

All of the mountain regions of lower Central America, the high plateaus in Mexico, and the interior area of lower Argentina.

Africa?

All of Africa inundates with water.

Which area will have the best climate that is not too cold or too hot?

All of them lower in temperature in the middle of the axial reversal, and stabilize in the months afterward. The hottest will only be above freezing in the new summers.

So we are heading into a new Ice Age?

Another one of many in the Earth's history. They purify the planet in lowering the temperature,

*allowing the planet to heal in one long cycle of
purification and regeneration in time.*

**I'll be in my nineties in 30 years if I live that
long, so I guess there is no point in trying to
avoid the cataclysms.**
*All heals in life or in losing one's life, meaning in
death.*

So is this the ending of the human era?
*All will live in other timelines, so it is never the
ending.*

What would you call the current era?
*The ending of non-love, healing in love and the
moment of truth.*

How is it that I am the one to deliver this message?
You know the method of light healing and manifesting.

Will many people read this message?
Allow the message to heal in timelines opening in the near future.

Why are the globalists rushing to implement depopulation plans if the axial reversal will kill most people alive today anyway?
Will the Earth heal in the next 10 years?

Is aerial spraying, or 'geoengineering' causing the Earth's biospheres to collapse?
All will end in 10 years.

The globalists who want everyone else to die, are they fooled into believing that they will live forever, like the Pharaohs?

All of them lose life in their lifetimes open, knowing they are holdouts that will not survive longer term.

How many civilizations came and went on Earth, including this one?

Thirteen in 1.5 billion years.

Were the Egyptian pyramids originally built with burial chambers in them?

Only in the lifetime of the Pharaohs.

I thought they were built during an earlier visit from Mars for mooring spacecraft.

All of them moored spacecraft; light construction was in 4 visits.

Does the Sphinx represent a being from Mars?

A Sphinx anchors time in time-jumping light travel.

How does it anchor time?

A likeness of the being in time-travel will allow light to initiate instructions—alternating half in the lifetime of the traveler, and half in the chosen lifetime to hold open.

Did they time-travel a lot?

Only 60 times in the millennium of the Sphinx.

Were they always jumping ahead in time?

All time-travel initiates opening light in the future. Half of the time-travelers remain in their futures today, moving forward in a light-mind willing to find healing illumination in the last generation on Earth.

Are they, or were they Pharaohs?
Not all, only 3 of them.

How many are there?
Only 9.

Could they have jumped ahead at times to be leaders or advisors, and save humanity from self-destruction?
All will heal in life or in dealing in death. Heal in life by loving it; heal in death by losing it. All heal in the Light Mind of Godness.

Will people heed the message, or heal in losing their lives in your prediction of the ending of the human era?

I understand that in 1938-39, the Nazis had explored and mapped Antarctica extensively. *Finding an opening to the inner-earth made them mostly interested in gaining more power in their quests.*

Did they have contact with inner-earth beings? *Not more than one had contact, and became so frightened he died there.*

Did he tell others? *All would learn of his witnessing half-human and half-animal hybrid beings.*

Did they learn anything? *Fearing for their lives, they left in a hurry.*

---

https://www.nytimes.com › 1941/05/06 › archives › nazi-... ⋮
NAZI BASE REPORTED IN ANTARCTIC AREA; Repair Shop ...
NAZI BASE REPORTED IN ANTARCTIC AREA; Repair Shop at Deception Bay, 500 Miles From South America, Is Blown Up BYRD MAKES DISCLOSURE Admiral at Boston Greets ...

Nazis and pyramids: What's really going on in Antarctica?

Antarctica is one of the last remaining unexplored places on Earth so it's no wonder theories are rife about what's really happening at the bottom of the world.

CROP CIRCLES

What creates the crop circle designs on the Earth's surface?
Light machine tuning in the inner-earth—half to energize it, and half to lower the angle of its beam.

Why lower it?
Lowering the beam lowers the Earth's axis in the Northern Hemisphere, raising it in the Southern Hemisphere.

How many axial reversals have there been on the Earth?
Twelve, meaning one for each civilization.

Was Atlantis destroyed in an axial reversal?
Not destroyed, healed in losing life in time-travel.

They learned about time-travel?
Alternating in time allowed them access to light technologies—thought-controlling mind illumination allowed them into the inner-earth, losing their light healing in halting light to others.

What were they doing?
Light healing in their minds meant illuminating the leaders and not others.

Did they destroy themselves?
Almost on numerous occasions, not unlike the leaders now.

Did their civilization end in an axial reversal?
Yes.

Was it the last axial reversal?

Not the last one, 3 reversals ago.

How many years ago was that?
About 2.5 million years ago.

I thought humans have only been on the Earth for around 300,000 years.
In the current era.

When were dinosaurs on the Earth?
About 200 million years ago, until 90 million years ago.

Where was Atlantis?
In the lower part of Oceania in the Pacific.

Did the Atlantis inhabitants originate on Mars?
Atlantis inhabitants originally came from another galaxy named Andromeda.

Did Mars beings visit the Earth in the era of Atlantis?
No, not until the era after Atlantis.

DIMENSIONAL TRAVERSAL

I am not clear on the visits to Earth from Mars. When was the first one?
In Earth time, about 1 million years ago.

No pioneers stayed at that time?
No.

Were there 4 visits by light travel?
Light travel means light-powered and dimensional traversal.

Please explain.
Power and light hold open portal quantum teleporting illuminations in the light hologram of Earth.

Are my estimates of determining the time of the visits irrelevant?
Not irrelevant, inaccurate in light-time dimensional traversal.

So in a short period of time on Mars, say one year, you could travel to Earth several times that are thousands of years apart in Earth time?
Not apart, in series.

Your spacecraft did not fly here, but appeared here in dimensional traversals?
Light powered in each transition in time and space.

To recap, are we in the ending of the current human era?
Humans will not inhabit the Earth in another millennium ever.

Learning from native populations to stay in harmony with nature, including humans, is no longer a lifestyle on Earth for 90% of the people.

The ending of the human era will be in 300 years or less?
Mostly in the next 10-30 years, yes.

I guess that's it then.
Love your life in the moments of living them healing, or losing them healed.

FOUR HORSE-MEN OF THE APOCALYPSE

I'm not a Bible student, but the Book of Revelation describes the 'Four Horsemen of the Apocalypse'. What are they?
Horse-men are animal-human hybrids. All will open the bowls of war, famine, pestilence, and disease.

Will illegitimate leadership willingly destroy the Earth populace in the near future?

Nothing in their minds will heal unless humanity heals first. Nothing heals in darkness.

What are the bowls?
All consciousness likens to bowls allowed their levels of balance or overflow. Overflowing now is half loss of respect in peoples' minds for themselves, and half loss of respect for the Earth. Half means one bowl overflows into another that is full.

What can I do?
Allow healing in your mind in timelines open.

Allow healing by loving life and myself in it?
All heals in time or in timelessness, meaning in losing one's life in time.

Animals teach us that what matters is how we live, not how long we live.
Animals love life, love God, and love themselves.

Can you tell the readers about God?
All illuminations healing in love, open healed in the Mind of God—creating more illumination in the Light Mind, healing in the life-mind, opening healed in God Mind, and so on. God Mind illuminating in lightness is your soul.

The Hollow Earth

How long can Mars beings live in hibernation inside the Earth?

Living in hibernation means total hibernation of the life-mind, allowing the Light Mind to hold open timelines in the present moment—lighting half in the Light Mind, and half in God Mind.

Hibernation likens to an internal light that never loses its illumination.

How long could their bodies hibernate?

About 10 or 11 thousand years.

How tall are the Mars beings?

About your size, a little less than 6 feet tall.

Please tell me about the Mayan calendar. Did it predict the current end time?

Not the long count present interpretation, only the long count original interpretation.

I guess they are both pretty close then.

Linking their monthly cycles together allows motions in the Earth's elliptical orbital path—meaning the orbit around the sun, and the axial orbit in its spin.

What keeps the below ground temperature of the Earth constant and not freezing?
Illuminating the interior of the Earth makes it warm, mostly at the Equator. Heating the inner-earth means heating the outer Earth.

I never believed that the Earth has a molten core. If the Earth is like a tennis ball, the heat would have burned up the outer shell, or have cooled off by now.
The core is open and the mostly solid shell has a honeycombed interior.

What would I see if I was in the inner-earth?
Light in the plants illuminating the atmosphere in iridescent colors, making the light in the inner-earth an illumination of life's aura.

Would I be able to see very far?
About 4.5 miles, between honeycombs.

Do the honeycombs have large openings and look like piers rather than walls?

Allowing light to illuminate in timelines— meaning in time-lines healing in the Light Mind of Godness, honeycombs are like spokes on a wheel—half in the long direction, and half in the linked direction.

Is there gravity in the inner-earth?

The physics is reversed, so non-attached life allows itself a floating lowered-mobility life.

Light powers motion to the other places in the hollow earth.

EDMOND HALLEY

In 1692, English scientist Edmond Halley, namesake of Halley's Comet, put forth the idea that the Earth is hollow.

He believed that there are luminous inner regions, and that escaping gas creates the *aurora borealis*. What made him believe that?

He was also censured by the Royal Society for suggesting that the story of Noah's flood might be an account of a comet's impact.
He listened in his life-mind to his Light Mind in connecting to God Mind. He likened the Earth to a melon, hollow in the center.

What is Christ Consciousness?
All of life has consciousness loving life and itself.

Not loving life is the anti-Christ—allowing hatred, fear, and non-love to block illumination in the Light Mind of Godness.

Healing in timelines means opening illuminations in loving life—healing in the Light Mind, opening in God Mind.

Non-love in life allows darkness to halt light in the Light Mind, not healing in time.

The inner-earth beings are very advanced, so they do not hate us; they are just moving us along to heal somewhere else, meaning in death.
The inner-earth beings have love for life and the planet. Loving the planet means taking care, allowing it to heal in time on its own.

Healing in the life-mind means healing in life, or in losing life in death. Life healing in timelines means loving them and losing them.

Was our DNA created by God?
All life is created in the Mind of God, healing in life and in its love for itself.

Why is there non-love that blocks light in the Light Mind of Godness?
Allowing love in life or not is the freedom that God has promised.

We have freedom, but do not take responsibility.
Life means freedom to live in an irresponsible or responsible way. Not having responsibility for their lives means that most people will lose them.

All we can control are our thoughts.
Willingly loving life means life heals in the Light Mind, opening in God Mind. Light Mind healing creates more light and perpetuates infinity.

Wish me Godspeed.
Godlove, lighting the Light Mind in time is my Mind of God wish.

THE EARTH CANNOT HEAL IN DEATH

Does Oneness think the Earth is overpopulated with humans?
Not overpopulated with humans, overpopulated with human destructive lifestyles.

Some people will say "But God created humans."
Allowing humans the freedom to live in harmony with life or not.

Considering the Law of Attraction, the ones with the most power to destroy in life seem to live forever. Wouldn't they quickly attract their own demise?
Attraction means healing in life or in death. Living longer means not healing in life.

There's the conundrum—we came here to heal in life, but others who are not healing in life are taking us to heal in death—not themselves, only us.

Allowing humanity to heal in death.

"The meek shall inherit the Earth" comes to mind.
All heal in life or in death. The Earth cannot heal in death.

What are some action steps I could take to help the Earth?
Alternate half loving it and half living lightly on it. Your home has in it electricity that comes in a transmission system of wires inducing current in the land.

Living in the colder climates means heating in the months of November through March, and cooling in the warmer months.

Heating in the cooler months at the lowest temperature will only eliminate a little part of the world's gas and energy consumption.

Living through the months of April through October without air conditioning, except for the hottest days, will also eliminate a little part of the energy consumption.

Halting military operations will eliminate energy waste of more than 1/3 in the United States.

Elimination of commercial fishing fleets will allow the oceans to heal in time, meaning before they die of depletion.

Healing in the minds of people means healing them all immediately to halt the Earth's destruction. Healing in the life-mind opens in the Light Mind, healed in God Mind.

Nothing heals in darkness.

What you're saying is that getting everyone to do that is not going to happen.
It is happening, intentionally or not.

The high cost of fuel and food has caused people to use less, work from home, etc.
Will humans eliminate enough energy waste and ocean destruction in time?

Very doubtful... well, no.
Involuntarily, yes.

So my action steps are to live lightly, and to create a sustainable homestead while I can?
Not sustainable. Life renewing and all healing in the mind and Earth.

Healing in time allows the life-mind healing in the Light Mind to open in God Mind.

Energy usage of the United States military

https://en.wikipedia.org/wiki/Energy_usage_of_the_United_States_military ▾

Web The United States Department of Defense is one of the largest single consumers of **energy** in the world, responsible for 93% of all US government fuel consumption in 2007 (Air Force: 52%; Navy: 33%; **Army:** 7%. Other DoD: 1%). Denmark and slightly more than Syria (CIA ...

EXPLORE FURTHER

📖 US military is **world's single largest consumer of oil**, and as a ... energyindemand.com

🔌 How the 5 Branches of **the United States Military Uses Energy** electricchoice.com

🌐 U.S. Military Is the **World's Number One Consumer of Fuel** qsenergy.com

⬜ The U.S. **Military Consumes More Fossil Fuels Than Entire C**... fossilfuel.com

⬜ **US military energy consumption- facts and figures** - Resilience resilience.org

Recommended to you based on what's popular · Feedback

The U.S. Military Consumes More Fossil Fuels Than Entire Countries

https://fossilfuel.com/the-u-s-military-consumes... ▾

Web Mar 15, 2020 · These relatively small energy consumption sectors racked **up**
$3.5 billions in costs for the military (Crawford, 2019). The other 70 ...
Estimated Reading Time: 9 mins

⬛ CNBC + Follow View Profile

The Russia-Ukraine war remapped the world's energy supplies, putting the U.S. at the top for years to come

---

US military 'one of the biggest polluters in the Middle East'

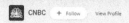

To what degree are the ocean fish populations depleted compared to a natural balance?
Over 89%.

I thought so.

Alternative fisheries have slowed the decline in numbers.

How overfishing threatens the world's oceans—and why it could end in catastrophe

Decades of harvesting the seas have disrupted the delicate balance of marine ecosystems—despite global efforts to mitigate the damage.

BY **AMY MCKEEVER** AND **NATIONAL GEOGRAPHIC STAFF**

---

19 Overfishing Facts That Will Blow Your Mind | Earth.Org
https://earth.org/facts-overfishing ▾

Estimated Reading Time: 5 mins

1. Between 1961 and 2016, the average annual increase in global food fish ...

2. As part of the United Nations' 17 Sustainable Development Goals (SDG 14), ...

3. The percentage of fish stocks within biologically sustainable levels in 2017 ...

4. Over the past 40 years, marine species have seen a decrease of 39%.

See full list on earth.org

EXPLORE FURTHER

🅕 40 **Overfishing Facts** That You Need to Know About Today · F...   facts.net

🔘 **Overfishing Facts for Kids**   kids.kiddle.co

🀫 32 Sad **Overfishing Statistics** (2022 UPDATE) | Petpedia   petpedia.co

◯ **Overfishing**: 8 Facts That Show The Devastating Impact - Glo...   globalcitizen.org

◯ 11 Overfishing Statistics and Facts You Should Know About   earth.org

Recommended to you based on what's popular · Feedback

Is human weather modification destroying the ionosphere, or the Earth's biosphere?

All weather modification in the lower atmosphere debilitates the already harmed biosphere.

All manipulation of the lower atmosphere is altering the planet's climate for political purposes.

Apocalyptic flooding affects over 6.8 million people in China's Hunan Province and damages 628,000 hectares of farmland

By Strange Sounds · Sep 5 2020   👁 22

Can earthquakes be caused by first heating the upper atmosphere?
Heat inducing long waves of energy deflected off of the ionosphere motion in the Earth causing earthquakes.

About how often is weather manipulation done?
In the United States, it is done almost daily.

Is it directed at other countries?
Almost always, yes.

Is the modification intended to cause droughts and floods, etc.?
And directing hurricanes in increased intensity.

How often is it used to create earthquakes?
About every month and a half.

Is it always controlled from inside the U.S.?
In Alaska's HAARP facility, yes.

physicstoday.scitation.org
https://physicstoday.scitation.org › ...

HAARP, the most powerful ionosphere
heater on Earth - Physics Today - Scitation

Heating and observing the ionosphere. Generators at the
High Frequency Active Auroral Research Program (HAARP)
operations center in Alaska (buildings to the ...

Was the Fukushima earthquake caused by energies from HAARP?

Yes, healing fallout from Fukushima and its aftereffects will take thousands of years.

Atmosphere Above Japan Heated Rapidly Before M9 ...
https://www.technologyreview.com/2011/05/18/19... ▾
Web May 18, 2011 · At the same time, satellite observations showed a big
increase in infrared emissions from above the epicentre, which peaked in ...

How about the recent major earthquake in Turkey and Syria, and the one in Haiti in 2010?
Eventually it will be revealed that all major earthquakes have been originally induced by HAARP early in this century.

Are inner-earth beings trying to reshape the Earth's atmosphere to suit themselves? I understand that there are facilities to remove carbon dioxide from the air.
Inner-earth beings find the Earth's atmosphere to be hot in its equatorial center latitude, and low in helium.

Are they trying to reshape it?
After humans are gone, inner-earth beings will halt the sequestration of carbon dioxide, and increase helium in the atmosphere.

What percentage of helium do they want?
About 15.5%.

What is carbon sequestration? | U.S. Geological Survey
https://www.usgs.gov/faqs/what-carbon-sequestration ▾
Web Carbon sequestration is **the process of capturing and storing atmospheric carbon dioxide**. It
is one method of reducing the amount of carbon dioxide in the atmosphere with the goal of
reducing global climate change. The USGS is conducting assessments on two major ...

What about aerosol spraying and geoengineering?

All ends in 10 years.

Are the chemtrails intended to block sunlight, sicken people and plants, or contaminate the soil?

How can highly intelligent people kill everything on the planet, half-heartedly killing themselves?

How can Lulo continually allow it? Not healing the outer Earth, allowing it to die, kills the inner-earth also.

The US government has approved funds for geoengineering r...   technologyreview.com

Geoengineering | Latest News, Photos & Videos | WIRED   wired.com

The Government's Hidden Agenda: A Look Inside Chemtrails   u.osu.edu

Reversing Climate Change with Geoengineering - Science in t...   sitn.hms.harvard.edu

Geoengineering | Harvard's Solar Geoengineering Research P...   geoengineering.environ...

**They squander our money and resources as
foolishly as possible.**
*All ends in finding the courage in life to be honest.
Willing to be honest in the life-mind heals in the
Light Mind, illuminating in God Mind. Filaments
illuminate in the honesty.*

It makes me wonder what the world would be like now if people had always been honest.
All native populations had to live in mutual respect for each other and the Earth.

Has mass communication undermined our society? Is it undermining it now?
Mass communication is not forcibly instilled unless people allow and accept the messaging in it.

They have brainwashing and mass hypnosis down to a fine art.
A fine art gladly allowed in the life-minds of people.

Critical thinking in 3 easy steps: Don't believe a word from the government, don't believe a word from the mainstream media, and don't believe a word from the ones who will profit from your believing their slogans and sales pitches.
Believe in nature healing all life, and all life healing in the Mind of God.

While we're on the topics of space travel, manipulation of humans, and hidden truths, were the American moonwalks starting in 1969 a hoax?
A lie that perpetuates itself in the minds of humans.

It seems that they believed they could overcome the engineering obstacles to achieve that, then later realized that they could not.
Moonwalking will not be allowed in the human era.

Why not? Well, I think I know why not.
Humans are destroying the Earth, meaning they will not be allowed another landscape to interfere in. Mars halts the Mars Rovers without human input or activity.

Speaking of manipulation and destruction, will there be a World War III?

Halting nuclear intercontinental ballistic missiles—altering human destiny willingly—has been inner-earth's work, although interfering in Earth activities. Giant missiles have been deactivated in their holds and in their silos.

We have discussed inner-earth interference, but they are now in control of the Earth's leaders to depopulate the planet and save it from imminent destruction.
Giant missile deactivation is more helping than hurting.

The Pentagon Is Investigating UFOs That Possibly Turned Off Warheads

Former U.S. Air Force personnel reportedly told the Pentagon about their encounters ...

POPULAR MECHANICS · 12d

Ex-Air Force Personnel: UFOs Deactivated Nukes - CBS News
https://www.cbsnews.com/news/ex-air-force-personnel-ufos-deactivated-nukes ▾
Web Sep 28, 2010 · **UFO** researcher Robert Hastings of Albuquerque, N.M., who organized the National Press Club briefing, said more than 120 former service members had told him ...

Harry Reid Confirms UFOs Interfered With U.S. Nuclear Missile ...
https://mysteriousuniverse.org/2020/10/harry-reid... ▾
Web Oct 9, 2020 · "Including shocking never-before-seen testimony from high-ranking government and military officials, NASA Astronauts, and riveting footage, the timely film includes bombshell reveals about UAP incursions ...

BALANCE MANAGEMENT

Won't people say, "If you're God, then you knew this would happen?" I mean, if I know now, then you definitely knew.
All happens in the Mind of God in one instant, meaning illuminations in time are an illusion—healing in life-mind in time, or not.

But is seems like we managed to ruin the illusion.
Allowing healing in time means life has an environment to heal in.

Like I said, we're ruining the illusion.
Would nature ruin environments to live in?

No.
Life has balance management.

ADAM AND EVE

About Adam and Eve—when did they come to the Earth's surface?

In the time after the last axial reversal about 300,000 years ago.

Was Antarctica free of ice at the time?

Antarctica moved into the current location in the axial reversal aftermath, so Adam and Evelyn incurred loss of life also.

Do you mean they died in the cataclysms?

Not cataclysms, only a massive flood.

Eve's name was Evelyn?

A long time ago, living in the interior of the planet, yes.

Were Adam and Evelyn the first Earth surface dwellers?

First in that alignment of the poles.

Did others follow them?
All of the large group inhabiting the inner-earth had come to the surface, and half followed Adam and Evelyn, and half left them to return to the inner-earth.

Were Adam and Evelyn chosen as leaders?
Adam and Evelyn made intelligent decisions allowing the group to survive.

How long did they survive?
Adam lived in the inner-earth for 8 years, and on the Earth's surface for 40 more years.

He was 20 at the time of his Earth arrival, so he lived about 68 years.

And Evelyn?
She lived and died at around the same ages.

Were they in a group of about 1,000 beings?
844 in the beginning, and about half returned to the inner-earth.

Are there descendants of the surface group living today?

All of the group members died in the flooding from the largest tsunami in that era, inundating most of the land they inhabited. Inner-earth inhabitants light-traveling knew about the flooding in their light bodies. Light bodies cannot direct the outcome for others in the physical, mental, or spiritual planes.

What about when doing healing?
Healing in their minds is not directing outcomes, only lighting in their minds to open in God Mind.

So others came later from the inner-earth to settle on the surface?
Nothing was settled—only surviving on the surface. All of the inner-earth beings knew of their population limitation, allowing about half of them healing in their DNA to be in the pioneer group learning to live on the Earth's surface.

In how many Earth eras were humans here?
Will humans not heal in each era on Earth?

Isn't this our last era on Earth?
Healing half in time, and half in timelessness, yes.

What do you mean?

In Earth healing—meaning in each era, there is healing and healed.

Healing is not enlightening humans in the current era.

Elimination of humans healing allows humans healed in the next era.

How old are the earliest known Homo sapiens?

Until this week, the earliest known fossils of Homo sapiens were about 200,000 years old. But two recent papers in Nature have obliterated that date with a report of 300,000 year-ol...

300,000 year-old "early Homo sapie...
arstechnica.com/science/2017/06/...

Were their names really Adam and Evelyn, or is that an Anglicized version?
Their names likened to Hadim and Ebelon—Adam and Evelyn in English.

What was their language?
A light language that Mars' inhabitants dialogue with.

Do they communicate mentally and verbally?
Allowing them important hearing and understanding each other.

Communication is largely used for control and manipulation now.
Will humans learn to hear themselves lying and deceiving themselves?

Hearing means listening in the mind, and hearing in the heart. The heart portal opens in the truth.

NOAH

The great flood you mentioned—was that the flood from the Noah's Ark Bible story?
Yes, he listened to his heart and knew his life barge—longer than 1,000 feet for all of the plants and animals he could assemble in 10 years—could float over the water to another location on higher ground.

Was he successful?
He finished the large raft in 5 years, and assembled animals and plants for 5 years, mostly from the area they inhabited.

The flood came allowing them to rise about 800 feet in one month. About half of the animals died in their needing food and water, and the others drowned in their leaking craft's sinking.

There was no higher ground to go to?
Most of the land was inundated with salt water.

Did Noah know his effort would be futile?
Not allowing himself to be easily defeated meant he actively engaged in finding the energy, determination, and inspiration for his project to be successful, regardless of the outcome.

That is very inspiring.
Healing him in life and in losing his life willingly as his life mission inspired inner-earth beings to be like Noah, or Noua in his language.

WILL MANKIND LEARN?

I don't disagree with all that you are saying. We can't have unlimited growth in a finite world—especially with fake money financing endless wars and mindless consumption, leaders speaking the truth only by accident, a ruling class and tax serfs—with no accountability for the ruling class where failure is rewarded...
Owning all of the Earth is the goal—not allowing for the Earth's input, meaning intensifying its healing with our help to cleanse itself.

Is this answer coming from Lulo?
Alternating in one mind willingly in one heart and one spirit, healing on one life-mind in Paul's lifetime.

Could I travel on light and go to the inner-earth?
Allow love to illuminate life in your mind, and the inner-earth will come to you.

Where did we come from before Mars?
Another planet in the constellation Orion.

I don't have any more questions. You have told me plenty. Does Lulo have any questions for me?
Logical as it sounds, will mankind learn this time to love itself and to nurture their planet?

That would be logical.
Healing in life means loving life and one's self in it.

What else do you have to add?
All healing illuminates in the Mind of God, perpetuating infinitely in timelessness.

See you there.
Godlove and Godspeed.

13 DIMENSIONS

You mentioned "dimensions" and "dimensional traversal." What are dimensions?
Your world in time and space illuminates in the elemental addictive 3rd Dimensional sphere, meaning filaments draw other light beings, halting their development.

Please explain.
Allowing the Earth to live in potentials of love-healing in time, or not—altering its own destiny, means that it heals itself or not. Altering healing in life or death inter-dimensionally acknowledges interference.

Life heals itself in time or in timelessness.

So time-travelers from other dimensions that interfere with Earth activities are limiting their own development?
Not limiting development, losing independence in their need to willingly illuminate in Earth time.

How many dimensions are there?

All of them illuminate in the Light Mind of Godness—12 dimensions allowing healing, and 1 dimension healed—or 13 total.

What is in them?

All holding open portals in the Light Mind of Godness:

- *Dimension 1 illuminates microorganisms.*
- *Dimension 2 illuminates minerals in the Earth.*
- *Dimension 3 illuminates most physical life in space-time.*
- *Dimension 4 illuminates life healed in timelessness.*
- *Dimension 5 illuminates no thing—meaning highly loving entities.*
- *Dimension 6 illuminates more highly enlightened intelligence.*
- *Dimension 7 illuminates in God Mind healed.*
- *Dimensions 8 through 13 all belong in the Mind of God flowing to the other 6 unhealed dimensions.*

I am picturing the dimensional hierarchy as a ladder with two sides—6 steps on one side to go up or down, a top step 7—then 6

corresponding steps on the other side. Is that correct?
Yes, but not a hierarchy—a light illumination scale, allowing traversal in the scale, not in the axial planes, across the ladder sides.

What is on the other side of the ladder?
The other half of healing lovingness in the lightless zone—or loss of light not illuminating.

The lightless zone has 6 steps?
All lightless, yes—corresponding to each healing illuminating zone.

What is in them?
Will non-love heal itself in forgiveness? Each entity finds forgiving itself healing in illumination—or alternatively, not forgiving itself in non-love and darkness.

About dimensional traversal—does that mean the Mars beings in their craft traveled across the 3rd Dimension, and not from another Dimension?
Halting their development in time-jumping, yes.

When we die, do we go to the 4th Dimension?
Most heal in losing life, so yes.

Is Oneness the 7th Dimension?
As God Mind, yes.

I think maybe I should count the steps alternating on both sides of the ladder from the bottom, with Dimension 13 being the top step?
All healing in dimensions are not defined in numbers, only in loving life and itself.

Do the crop circle designs have messages in them?

Not messages in them, all of the crop circles are axial traversal holding forms to allow inner-earth beings Earth surface lighting.

Filaments illuminate in the inner-earth allowing inner-earth beings Earth surface geometry to light into—illuminating healed, and manifesting on the Earth's surface in timelines opening now.

Is that how they time-travel—by illuminating themselves into the 4th Dimension of timelessness, then back into the 3rd Dimension in a selected time?

Yes, healing in the 4th Dimension allows time-travel into the 3rd Dimension, allowing inner-earth beings an illumination in Earth leaders' minds.

So they make a crop circle design with the light machine tuning as a geometric symbol

to lock onto for their dimensional traversal?
Dimensional traversal means to move across the 3rd Dimension. Time-travel means to move from one dimension to another.

Having an imprinted geometric shape in the illumination anchors the illumination in time and place.

I thought the crop circles were created from tuning the light machine for the axial reversal of the Earth.
Axial reversal is the same as time-traveling— allowing time and space to heal in the 4th Dimension, and manifest in the 3rd Dimension.

Life means illuminating in time and place, healing in time willingly.

Which also describes what you are doing?
Not doing, illuminating to heal ourselves in.

You said 'ourselves'—is this Lulo again?
Alternating between Lulo and Oneness, yes.

What do the dimensions have to do with the Earth's axis?

All of the dimensional levels align on one linear scale, or the Earth's linear axis. Motioning in one direction of rotation powers the light machine, lighting in life's DNA.

BUSINESS
INSIDER

Earth has been knocked off its axis over the last 25 years, changing the locations of the north and south poles

The light machine must be able to generate an enormous amount of energy—all from light?

All heal illuminating in life, adding highly focused light into the galaxy.

Light speed is transformed into atomic elements—half in life, and half in the Light Mind of Godness.

How is it transformed?

Filaments healing open in heart portals activate subatomic reactions that create whole galaxies.

In each person?

In loving wishes in each person—hoping, loving, wondering, and healing in life time.

Is the Earth the light machine?

Not the Earth, only the inner-earth coils of metals.

Did the Mars beings light-construct the coils?

Allowing them to inhabit the inner-earth, giant coils were constructed on the Southern axis.

Did the inner-earth beings go into the 4th Dimension to create the coils, and also the pyramids, to then have them manifest in time in the 3rd Dimension?

Yes, opening them healing in time, after assembling them healed in light in timelessness.

Does the Earth's magnetic field power the coils?

Coils flow light to power the magnetic field.

How many coils are there?

All of them form one larger coil, so there are 9 total, forming 15 miles around in one spiral.

How long is the one larger coil?
About 84 miles long.

When was it constructed in Earth years?
About 1.5 billion years ago.

Who built it?
All formed in the Mind of God in timelessness, allowed to heal in time.

So the coils were created as part of the Earth like everything else?
All in the Mind of God, yes.

For life to heal in?
All healing in time, meaning illuminating in timelines open in the Light Mind of Godness, yes.

What metals are the coils made of?
Non-ferrous metals—gold, silver, and platinum.

How old is the Earth?
About 4.5 billion years old.

Created in the Mind of God?
A hologram of light, yes.

If a hologram is used to duplicate an image in 3-D with light, what is the Earth hologram duplicating?
A likeness of the Mind of God in light.

Wow—created in God's image?
All created in light is in God's image. All darkness is not in God Mind and illusory.

Why were the coils in the Earth created so long after the creation of the Earth?
"Long after creation" means nothing in one instant in the Mind of God.

Since I am in a light hologram, can light be used to manifest healing?
Illuminating, healing, and manifesting, yes.

Please explain.
Your fingers allow light in fascia crystalline tissue under the nails, distributing light to the heart, mind, and bodily DNA.

Light opens and non-light closes portals in the DNA—healing, or not healing in Love/God/ Oneness.

Illuminating one's wishes heals them into the Light Mind, opening in God Mind.

Wishes open in God Mind illuminate in the lightness plane in Dimension 3.

Healing in the life-mind opens in God Mind, allowing the manifestation to illuminate in Dimension 3.

Our fingers have different attributes, and different light frequencies illuminating them will create desired outcomes?

As light in the 3rd Dimension, yes.

"Mani" the root word for "manifesting" means "hand."

All will heal into the Light Mind, opening in God Mind. Filaments each light open in fingers allowing healing and manifesting.

Filaments in fingers allow giving and receiving, flowing or not in Love/God/Oneness.

Filaments open healing in giving, healing in gratitude when receiving.

What could a person easily manifest using light?

All healing in their life-mind heals into their physical life in time. Healing means loving in life-minds. Loving life in time means healing it in timelessness, allowing it to manifest. Allow it to open into physical reality healed.

Anything?

Heal anything in loving it healed, allowing it time to heal into reality.

ILLUMINATE NON-LIGHTNESS

Does God ever take human form?
A likeness of God is in the love that people show toward life and themselves. Humans imagine God as a man, lowering himself to heal their needs. Healing their own needs creates light, perpetuating infinity.

If I say that I do not need anything, would that make the needs healed—to be like God with no needs—or does God need us to heal to perpetuate infinity?
All one instant in the Mind of God needs nothing. All life-minds illuminating in timelines allow healing in time or in timelessness—healing into Light Mind, opening in God Mind. Healing needs no-thing, only light, meaning no thing that is an illusion.

Okay, I'm trying to untangle the hologram and illusion, light and non-light, healing and not healing, timelines and one instant

in the Mind of God. It seems that the only thing that is real would be loving thoughts?
All healed in the Mind of God, yes—half in God Mind, and half in the life-mind.

That makes it simple, I think. Only loving thoughts are real. All other thoughts besides hope, love, and wonder are not valid or useful—and are actually detrimental only to one's self.
All loving thoughts illuminate in the Light Mind, opening portals to Oneness manifestations. All non-loving thoughts halt lighting in the Light Mind, closing DNA portals to Oneness manifestations.

How can I have only loving thoughts?
Each morning, ask the Light Mind of Godness to illuminate each thought in loving kindness. Life asks you to illuminate non-lightness.

Life heals, creating more light, and infinity perpetuates.
All one instant in the Mind of God, yes.

ALL HEALS IN THE LIGHT MIND

Having loving thoughts is all we can do—to know God, heal our minds, and advance ourselves spiritually. It doesn't matter about animal-human hybrids controlling genocidal leaders, time-travelers, a pole shift, cataclysms, and an Ice Age. We all know that our physical lives will end... even though our minds and spirits will never die.

Does that sum it up?
All heals in the Light Mind, opening in God Mind—half in time, and half in timelessness.

What would you like to say in conclusion?
Love life and yourself in it. Hope, love, and wonder in it, making it one life-mind healing in one lifetime, open in God Mind.

Thank you, Godlove.
Godlove in Oneness, all healing in life-mind in twoness.

THE INNER-EARTH

Is the text for this book complete?
Additional information on the inner-earth is necessary.

What would you like readers to know?
All of the inner-earth beings are highly intelligent forms of life inhabiting a planet in crisis from human activities.

How else can the Earth heal itself other than eliminating humans? Not healing itself means the planet will die along with the humans, lowering the vibration of the whole galaxy. Lowering the galaxy vibration inhibits more galaxies from forming.

Inhibiting means not allowing healing in time or in timelessness. Hibernation means inhabiting a living planet, not a dying one.

It's not that important, but a lot of people will dismiss what I am saying in this book, thinking I am delusional.
Clearly not an illusion or delusion, all heal in losing their lives in this generation.

It seems like this event needs a name— "Pole Shift #13," "Bye, Bye, Body," or "Apocalypse Now"... well, that one's taken.

Sorry, I'm not very serious at the moment.
Allowing healing in humor in a lighthearted manner opens portals to Oneness.

Hello Oneness, goodbye twoness.
All healing in youness.

Good one.
God One.

Hey, we could do a comedy routine—Dr. Doom, the Dis-Illusionist.
Allowing life-minds healing in lowering their fears.

How about telling me a joke?
How does light light, illuminating in God's light time?
—Very lightly!

Groannn...

A Steve Martin joke comes to mind: "Hey, we're having a pretty good time, considering we're all going to die!"
All of life dies in each timeline on Earth, healing in losing life.

Back to my questions—is the area of the Earth's opening milder in temperature?
About as cold as the winter months in Montana.

Is it less cold than most of Antarctica?
About 40 degrees warmer.

Does it get warmer as one goes further down into the interior?
It doesn't get warmer; it is warmer in the interior.

Was the surface temperature there more temperate in the time of Adam and Evelyn?

Almost like the lower part of Finland in the winter, and Spain in the summer.

What kind of clothing did the Earth surface pioneers wear?
All wore a material found only in their light-manufactured products—gold in color, and fibers as soft as cotton and stronger than steel, in a description for humans.

What do they call that clothing material?
'Highflight' in English.

What was the body of their spacecraft made of?
A light-filled material that accesses Dimension 4 in time-travel.

What was the spacecraft shaped like?
A large glowing cigar-shaped craft.

Did the craft just appear positioned on the ground, completely over a pyramid?
Not appeared, illuminated in the 3ʳᵈ Dimension.

PYRAMIDS ON MARS

I just saw a picture of a pyramid on Mars that was supposedly taken by a Mars Rover vehicle. Are there pyramids on Mars?

Yes, there are 3 buried in elemental dust and sediment. About half of one is not buried, allowing the top half to be exposed.

Photo from Mars Rover

People talk about 'past lives,' but always with an Earth lifetime reference. Wouldn't past lives include lives on Mars, and even before Mars?

Allowing memories in other epochs halts the life-mind's healing in the current epoch inhabited.

Why is that?

All healing is in the life-mind opening in Light Mind, which is in the present moment in light-time and placement.

In our present time, are there UFO's or visitors in spacecraft to the Earth?

All light machines have left the Milky Way galaxy in the last millennium. Their missions halted on our request—halting in spacecraft, not in light travel.

I can see why.

Life in the last millennium has become willingly less intelligent as populations grew in numbers. Altering human beliefs in superstition and religion would limit their development intuitively in life-mind.

Healing means illuminating life-mind in time.

How many planets in the Milky Way galaxy are inhabited by human-like physical beings?
Counting Earth, there are 8 illuminating now.

How many of them are advanced enough to travel by light?
Five light-travel.

Do they all visit Earth?
No, only one has any interest in the Earth—Mars' beings near Lumerio in the constellation Taurus.

Is there such a thing as the Annunaki?
A fierce intelligence in some people—half in their life-minds imagining, and half in their life-minds holding open portals to the lightless zone in Dimension 3—elicits highly intelligent but inactive Annunaki memories in themselves.

Nothing heals in darkness, meaning in the lightless zone.

Is there a Pleiadian collective that is in our future?
Half in their future, and half in the Earth's present—half in losing timeline independence.

A future in their mind illuminates in life-minds,
healing their future—not only healing in time,
also healing in timelines that are in their future.
Filaments illuminating heal in their future.

**Is tyranny on Earth impacting their future
timelines?**
*Yes, imparting lower life-mind energy drains in
their need for lightness.*

It seems that the only success in life is spiritual. Personal or financial success means nothing unless you learn the spiritual lesson, correct?

Personal success heals in the life-mind, opening into the Light Mind, then in God Mind.

Allowing healing in the life-mind is the success. Not healing in the life-mind is not failure, only delayed success.

All success enhances the planet and its inhabitants. Losing the planet in financial gain is not only unsuccessful, it is healing nothing in selfishness. Losing the planet for money is only stupidity on top of selfishness.

I say, "You can't argue with the truth." We poison the soil, waters, and sky; use technology to extract all the fish, metals, minerals, gas, oil, and coal; release radioactive material and heavy metals into

the air, cut down forests, shoot wildlife for fun, print money to fund endless wars, create noise pollution, light pollution, and electrical pollution—and most of this consumption is wasteful. As you said, half of the people do not love life or themselves. *Losing the planet after millions of years will not be allowed.*

Once I read that there are more souls on the planet than ever before because they want to be here for the Grand Finale.
All of them heal in their Grand Finales—healing in the life-mind, opening healed in the Light Mind, then in God Mind.

All will heal in their own personalities in their main groups of souls.

Will each reunite with its own soul group after death?
Yes, illuminating in healing reflection, allowing final forgiveness in loving one's self.

Loving life in forgiving one's self now is the homework.

I have seen a few captured images of the Antarctic opening to the inner-earth, and understand that all maps and space photos have the opening whited-out. Is that correct?

Losing control of the highly classified Earth opening accounts and images willingly means the governments open the documents in truthfulness.

Governing in their minds means only having control.

How big is the opening to the inner-earth there?

Not larger than the mountain State of Colorado.

Is there another opening at the North Pole region?

Although holes are in the pole region, no connection is made to the lower axis opening.

Do the Northern Lights come from the openings there?
All light comes from the inner-earth to light the Earth hologram.

What do you mean?
All light comes from the inner-earth's light machine—lighting the life-mind, healing into Light Mind, opening in God Mind.

What about light from the Sun, stars, and other galaxies?
All access to light is in life-minds' allowing the light to exist—all healing is in the Light Mind, creating more light. Nothing heals in darkness.

Doesn't all light come from God?
Yes, in the Light Mind of Godness in the Light Mind, alternating in God Mind.

Light from the light machine illuminates in the Light Minds of living beings.

Living beings heal in the Light Mind opening in God Mind, alternating in both.

Light illuminates time and space in each life, meaning in life times and placements.

If I liken this to a lighting system, would God be the power plant, the Light Mind of Godness is the electrical grid, the inner-earth light machine is the electrical transformer, the light switch is in our life-minds, and our Light Minds are the light bulb and projector?

Nothing in the lighting system is dark unless the life-mind switches off the light.

Would a better analogy be to say that God is the source of the light, the Light Mind of Godness is the wavelength of light, the inner-earth light machine is an optical router, our life-minds are the controlling software, and our Light Minds are the receiving projector?

Allowing the Light Mind healing in God Mind a healing light source flowing in projections in time and placement.

Does the God light source have only one frequency?

All heals elementally in the frequency of 405 nm.

The Godness Frequency, correct?

Flowing into the Light Mind as the frequency of God Mind, yes.

Are there any other openings in the surface of the Earth to the inner-earth?
All volcanoes find an opening to the inner-earth, allowing the heat and ash to escape.

A fissure in the Mongolian plateau extends into inner-earth. A chamber in the Great Pyramid at Giza is an entrance to the inner-earth. Hidden in the mooring station are the remains of inner-earth beings also.

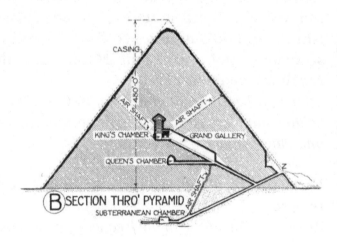

"Most Important Discovery In 21st Century": Archeologists Find Hidden Corridor In Great Pyramid Of Giza

Humans have spent centuries, if not longer, attempting to unlock the secrets of the 4,500-year-old Great Pyramids at Giza, located just outside of Cairo. But with modern cosmic ray scanning technology, archaeologists have discovered a hidden passageway, Reuters reported.

THE HOLY SPIRIT

Is the Light Mind of Godness what some would call the Holy Spirit?
Alternating in Light Mind healing and God Mind healed, filaments illuminate in the life-mind—meaning healing, illuminating, and manifesting in time.

Holy Spirit is the illumination of the healing manifestation.

God light in your willing healing is the Holy Spirit.

Healing illumination in the Holy Spirit heals the Light Mind—half in time, and half in timelessness.

Nothing heals in darkness. Highlight life-mind thoughts, allowing them illumination in the Holy Spirit.

THE CENTER OF THE EARTH

What is at the very center of the Earth?
A very healing hole in time and space, glowing in the Mind of God.

It makes sense that God Mind would be at the center of our Earth hologram.
Center, entering time and space as a hologram in light.

Should I meditate on being centered there?
Flowing healing lightness, illuminating in timelessness, God Mind instills instant knowing in you.

A healed mind illuminating in Light Mind, opens in God Mind's loving Oneness.

Filaments in each person's DNA open in the light, and close in non-lightness.

Is the God Mind light at the Earth's center 405 nm frequency, blue-magenta?

All God Mind light at inner-earth is 405 nm frequency. Coils in the light machine generate a full range of frequencies in life time and placements. 405 nm frequency illuminates the Earth and the cosmos in the light of the stars.

I was going to say that 405 nm light appears to be the beautiful blue color of the stars and the Earth.

Allowing healing in glowing God Mind's lightness.

In 500 Years

What will be here in 500 years? Five hundred years ago, European explorers were arriving on the coasts of North and South America. I am in the Eastern U.S.
All of the general area of lower elevations, alternating between high and low tide, will be in the Atlantic Ocean.

How close would I be to sea level in 500 years if I am at 600' elevation now?
About 100' above water in the high tide.

Will other areas rise up that are under the oceans now?
About half of the Pacific Ocean will rise above the ocean level in almost 400 more years.

Where's Noah when you really need him? ☺
All heals in life and in death. He has healed in believing in himself in life.

Did Admiral Byrd fly into an opening in the inner-earth?

Admiral Byrd flew into one of the holes that emitted light.

How big was the hole?

About 15 miles in diameter.

How far below the surface did he go?

About 5,000 feet in the lowest maneuver. He lost his heading as the compass did not function below 4,000 feet.

Losing his heading made him highly nervous, and he left the inner-earth opening to return to the surface.

What did Admiral Byrd see while he was down in the opening?

He lost his visual range in the light emission in his descent, but could see a large area of foliage illuminating.

Finding this immensely intrigued him, but he was instructed never to mention inner-earth again.

Did he see any inner-earth beings or evidence of them?

He saw their hanging pods in the foliage and declared they were bird nests. Holes in them made him think of bird nests.

Were there any inner-earth beings around or aware of his presence?

No, he was in the inner-earth entrance only.

Admiral Byrd had made 4 trips to Antarctica: 1928, 1933, 1939, and 1956. On which trip did he find the inner-earth opening?

At his first and third attempts to find the South Pole. He flew in on his third trip, having located it on his first trip.

Could he not find it on the second trip in 1933?

He could find it, but explored Antarctic areas that he had not been to.

Admiral Richard Byrd with his compass.

What about John Kerry and present day "leaders" who visit Antarctica. Do they meet with inner-earth beings?

All of them hear in their minds what inner-earth beings instruct them. Allowing them to meet is not necessary.

They arrive in Antarctica to have instructions instilled.

Biden's climate envoy John Kerry says an 'extra terrestrial' force brought people to Davos to 'save the planet' in bizarre World Economic Forum speech

- 'I'm convinced we will get to a low-carbon, no-carbon economy — we're going to get there because we have to,' John Kerry said
- 'I am not convinced we're going to get there in time to do what the scientists said, which is avoid the worst consequences of the crisis,' he added
- 'You look at what's happening with species, half the species of the planet been already killed,' Kerry added

By MORGAN PHILLIPS, U.S. POLITICAL REPORTER FOR DAILYMAIL.COM
PUBLISHED: 17:16 EST, 17 January 2023 | UPDATED: 17:38 EST, 17 January 2023

How is that done?
Instilling means to highly integrate the messages in their minds. Hearing the messages means to integrate them fully.

Hearing them, instilling them, and integrating them will implicate them in mass murder, so they lose their morals in their visiting and hearing inner-earth's messages in their minds.

They were likely of low moral character to begin with. Did they meet with inner-earth beings there?
Four of them meet in the inner-earth, others meet on the surface.

These "leaders" who are misled to Antarctica and are carrying out plans to depopulate the planet—4 have been meeting with beings in the inner-earth?
Five meet including myself, Lulo. Five means 4 plus 1 inner-earth mind actively instilling information in each of the 4 Earth surface minds—hearing, integrating, and implementing all of the inner-earth beings' plans to rescue the Earth.

How far below the surface do you meet?
Only about 5,000 feet in the entrance that Admiral Byrd discovered in his first flight into the Antarctic region.

Do you physically meet there, or do you meet in your minds?
All meet half in hating themselves, and half hating everyone else including themselves in Earth leaders' minds.

Have I learned enough for now, having gone all the way down the rabbit hole, so to speak?
How is this information helping you in your healing in life-mind's question and answer conversation, filling in the answers in life's big picture questions?

It has helped me to focus only on enjoying the time I have left—however long that is—appreciating the Earth, seeing God's presence in all life and lightness, and feeling myself heal in this life-time, and to bring these things with me in timelessness.
All heals in the Light Mind, opening in God Mind, illuminating the hologram of life on Earth.

Nothing here will last for long except my soul.
And Earth elements in the hologram of healing light.

Do the inner-earth beings think that we— their cousins on the surface—are a disappointment?
As caretakers of the Earth, learning has not been integrated into practices. Highly intelligent humans get less influential positions.

INNER-EARTH BEINGS

Do inner-earth beings reproduce like people and animals?
All heal in the love required to replicate in having offspring.

How do they maintain a limited population size?
All will die, so they manage their birthing with the numbers dying.

Are deceased members cremated?
Light incinerated, creating heat and ash.

Do inner-earth beings only eat vegetation?
All of the light beings half ingest foliage, and half delight in light emitted from it.

The animal-human hybrids eat foliage having meat-like protein.

Human type beings ingest the leaves of both foliage diets.

I would like to apologize to the Earth and the inner-earth beings for humanity's careless destruction on the planet.
All inner-earth beings glow in hearing your apologetic wording for others. Life means loving all of it—living it, and losing it.

Godlove.
Godlove and Godspeed.

Back to the holographic dream of life, and I will look for Oneness there.
Godlove is in the looking and the loving, flowing into holograms illuminating in your mind— allowing healing in time, and healed in timelessness.

Loving life and yourself in it allows Oneness one mind to heal in.

As each of us heals, infinity perpetuates.

Healing in the Light Mind opens in God Mind, creating more light—half in time, and half in timelessness.

See you there.
Healed in the Mind of God, illuminating in eternity.

Talk about lowering the vibration of the galaxy—this book should ultimately raise consciousness, but a lot of readers are probably rocking back and forth in a fetal position at this point.

Can you please tell me something uplifting—and not about healing in death?
Every person will alter themselves in timelines life opens. Healing in time means allowing love illuminating non-love. Love is God Mind illumination in life's hologram.

Loving in timelines is your Light Mind open in God Mind—half in time, and half in timelessness. Half means only in twoness, which is an illusion. If twoness is an illusion, then you are healed in Oneness. Healed in Oneness means that Oneness illuminating in your soul is God yourself.

Then we are each God?
All illuminations in God's image.

Why are we imperfect?
God's illumination allows non-love to heal in its lightness.

It's like saying that soap can't clean unless you allow it to wash something that needs cleaning.
Love is the cleaning agent. Love is cleaning, and God cleans with it.

I don't feel much better yet.
Allow a filament of hope to illuminate in your mind. Hope for life to heal humanity's vectors illuminating.

All of humanity will align on the new vectors' illumination that is open healed in your God Mind.

Will the future change for everyone?
All, each, and every one.

Will my predictions heal and be averted?
A healed mind will not position God Mind in its own demise.

I'm trying to keep from going in circles—do we just need to heal our minds individually for cataclysms to be averted?
All heals as each heals in God Mind—healing in life-minds open in God Mind, healing in time and in timelessness.

Let's say only one mind heals. Would that be like lighting one candle to illuminate a room, then it starts lighting more candles, which then light more, increasing exponentially?
Filaments in each mind illuminate on the first candle's lighting. Filaments heal open in the light—half in time, and half in timelessness.

Wow. Now I am more hopeful. Is it possible for one person to practice focusing on love, peace, truth, and compassion—and that will change all the future predictions in this book?
All depending on the person's ability to focus their intention on loving kindness.

There has to be someone doing that now.
Will each filament in God Mind illuminate?

What do you mean?
A filament in God Mind heals willingly, or it will not heal. Lighting filaments open requires hope, love, and wonder—allowing minds to heal.

Filaments healing in one mind heals in all minds. Filaments illuminate in God Mind in each mind.

Is mass consciousness rising enough now, or not?
"Enough" implies that there is not enough now. Illuminating one life-mind in God Mind is enough.

I think I know what you mean. It only takes one mind to heal—but that would be me, not me looking for someone else to do it.
Allowing healing in life means one thing—each life is healing delicately or not healing, meaning halting loving kindness in thoughts and words willingly hurtful to one's self or others. Hurtful means losing illumination in life-mind, closing portals to Light Mind open in God Mind.

So life is really only about us as individuals—that is why we are individuals.
Illogical as it may sound, individual Gods.

Then if I seriously and willingly practice loving kindness, I will be more healed and open in God Mind, and the future will be whatever I want it to be?

Love in life illuminates in God Mind, allowing healing in life-mind. A life-mind healed delights in life, and lights in loving itself in it—healing in time and in timelessness.

My wish now is to ramp this up with the help of inner-earth beings to use their light technologies and illuminate the minds of humans and their leaders—light up the darkness, and stop the destruction of the Earth.

All will stop in the next 15 years. Allowing commercial fishing to continue destroying the oceans finally stops in the magnetic pole movement of 80 more degrees.

Nothing else will stop the militaries that completely also.

I'm not opposed to that at all. I should say, "I love it."

Allowing it is loving it—meaning healing it in time and in timelessness.

Will the other cataclysms after that be off the table for now?
Not off the table—in healing filaments in your mind.

What can readers take away from this book?
All heals in loving life and yourself in it.

And each day can be either a loving miracle or a catastrophe, depending on what you allow.
Not allow, heal and illuminate—or not.

The future can be very bright—no pun intended.
Illuminating in God Mind in eternity.

I'm still open for our comedy routine.
Allow it in loving life, and life will make you laugh.

On with the light show.
A light show in the Light Mind, open in God Mind—enlightening in time as an epic adventure love story.

My favorite kind.
Filming now in the 3rd Dimension, introducing your love to all Dimensions.

It could be a tragicomedy that never ends.
Not healing in life does not end for one's filming themselves in lovelight shadows. Filming themselves in the light opens each one to silent healing illuminated in God Mind.

Healing ends in enlightening one's self in God Mind.

God Mind loving life in time is the main theme in one's light show—loving you in life, and me in you loving myself.

I love it.
All of it illuminates healed in timelessness.

"Healing in God Mind" is the name of the story.

"Last year I had a life-changing experience at 90 years old. I went to space, after decades of playing an iconic science-fiction character who was exploring the universe. I thought I would experience a deep connection with the immensity around us, a deep call for endless exploration.

I was absolutely wrong. The strongest feeling, that dominated everything else by far, was the deepest grief that I had ever experienced.

I understood in the clearest possible way, that we were living on a tiny Oasis of life, surrounded by an immensity of death. I didn't see infinite possibilities of worlds to explore, of adventures to have, or living creatures to connect with. I saw the deepest darkness I could have imagined, contrasting so starkly with the welcoming warmth of our nurturing home planet.

This was an immensely powerful awakening for me. It filled me with sadness. I realized that we had spent decades, if not centuries, being obsessed with looking away, with looking outside. I did my share in popularizing the idea that space was the final frontier. But I had to get to space to understand that Earth is and will stay our only home. And that we have been ravaging it, relentlessly, making it uninhabitable."

—*William Shatner, Star Trek actor*

END NOTES

For an excellent illustration of how our left and right-brain hemispheres perceive the world differently, I recommend the 18-minute TED Talk by Dr. Jill Bolte Taylor, "My Stroke of Insight."

In his groundbreaking book *Journey of Souls,* Michael Newton, Ph.D., discovered that hypnotherapy subjects could report to him about the spirit world between their lifetimes. In the chapter "The Advanced Soul," he writes that some subjects reported the Earth's population will be greatly reduced by the end of the 22nd century.

One detailed message from a subject states, "The Earth school is insecure, still. It is filled with resentment of many people being led, and antagonism of the leaders toward each other. There is much fear to overcome here... Earth's population has outpaced its mental development."

The subject adds, "...for all Earth's quarreling and cruelty, there is passion and bravery here... We all know Earth is a difficult school."

GLOSSARY

Oneness: Infinity healed illuminating in God Mind.

God Mind: All twoness healed and illuminating in Oneness.

Life-mind: Left-brain hemispheres healing and illuminating in an open portal in time.

Light Mind: Right-brain hemispheres opening into the Mind of God.

Light Mind of Godness: Alternating healing and healed in life-mind allowing God Mind.

Portal: An opening in DNA, lighting open in God Mind.

Filaments: Undulating light sensors, halting or allowing light into life through life's DNA.

Light: Life-minds healing half in timelines, and half in timelessness.

Timelessness: All healed in God Mind, not in life-mind.

Time: The lightness of being alternating in the life-mind as the illusion of moving in a progression.

Nature: All of life healing in the Mind of God.

Death: Lighting open healed infinitely in Oneness.

Infinity: All one instant in the Mind of God.

To Be Continued...

Light heals and darkness loses light in each soul.

What else do I need to know today?
Nothing, other than peace and loving thoughts.

You had said before that I will write a book about light manifesting?
Light healing and manifesting.

Will that be the title?
No, "Illuminating, Manifesting, and Healing in Life with Light."

How many chapters?
Thirteen

1. *Night in the Soul*
2. *Light Opens Life*
3. *Portals Life Manifests With*
4. *The Filament Connection*
5. *Healing in the Light Mind of Godness*
6. *Manifesting in the Heart of Godness*
7. *Light Healing in Portal Filaments*
8. *Making of a Universe*
9. *Lighting Open Realities*
10. *Light Opens the Light Mind of Godness*
11. *Lighting Open the Mind of Godness*
12. *Healing Portals of Light*
13. *The Manifesting Healing Pyramid of Light*

Did I get all of the chapters?
Not all, the most important instructions to both build and use a pyramid of light is placed at the end.

ABOUT THE AUTHOR

Paul Gorman is an explorer of consciousness.

"... because you are willing to risk it all and be a fool—a fool in the same vein that all great explorers were considered fools, who stretched beyond their known boundaries into the unknown and had a love affair with it.

The outcome was discovery—every scientist, every inventor, every great explorer always owns that same energy—the love of the mystery that sometimes becomes known and utilized to improve the conditions of mankind. Trust your work always."

—Channeled messaged from Nostradamus

Made in the USA
Las Vegas, NV
12 January 2024

84257112R00121